CAIRO

BY R. CONRAD STEIN

CHILDREN'S PRESS®
A Division of Grolier Publishing
New York London Hong Kong Sydney
Danbury, Connecticut

CONSULTANTS

Noha Aboulmagd Forster, M.A.
Ph.D. Candidate in Middle Eastern History
Princeton University

Linda Cornwell
Learning Resource Consultant
Indiana Department of Education

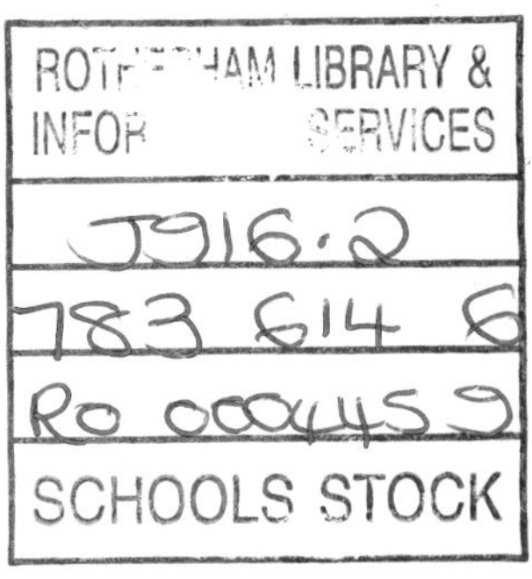

Project Editor: Downing Publishing Services
Design Director: Karen Kohn & Associates
Photo Researcher: Jan Izzo
Pronunciations: Courtesy of Ahmed Adala, Arabic Teacher, Master's student, Northeastern Illinois University; and Tony Breed, M.A. Linguistics, University of Chicago

NOTES ON ARABIC PRONUNCIATION

The pronunciations in this book are simplified because there are many sounds in Arabic that do not occur in English. Most pronunciations are exactly as they look, with the following notes: *th* is *th* as in thing; *th* (underlined) is *th* as in then; *ghee* is like the *gea* in gear. The *gh* in *ghah* is a sound that does not occur in English—it's a relaxed *g* sound, sort of a gurgling noise. The closest sound in English is *g* as in go.

Library of Congress Cataloging-in-Publication Data

Stein, R. Conrad.
Cairo / by R. Conrad Stein.
p. cm. — (Cities of the world)
Includes index.
Summary: Describes the physical characteristics, history, people, and customs of the capital city of Egypt.
ISBN 0-516-20024-0
1. Cairo (Egypt)—Juvenile literature. [1. Cairo (Egypt)]
I. Title. II. Series: Cities of the world (New York, N.Y.)
DT143.S64 1996 96-5950
962'.16—dc20 CIP

Printed in the United States of America.
1 2 3 4 5 6 7 8 9 10 R 05 04 03 02 01 00 99 98 97 96

TABLE OF CONTENTS

A LOOK AT THE EGYPTIAN

The Cairo Tower is the city's tallest building. From the deck on its top floor, a visitor looks down on a curious skyline: Ancient domes stand beside modern glass-and-concrete high-rises. On a clear day, the three great Pyramids of Giza are visible. They stand about 9 miles to the south. The pyramids are among the oldest structures on earth. Below the pyramids crouches the mysterious Sphinx. With the body of a lion and a human face, the Sphinx stares out into eternity.

Cairo (KIGH-ROE)
pyramid (PEER-UH-MID)
Giza (GEE-ZAH)
Sphinx (SFINKS)

Directly below the Cairo Tower flows the Nile River. Like many ancient cities, Cairo owes its existence to its river. For centuries, the Nile served as an avenue of trade for the inhabitants. The river was also a highway used by Egypt's many invaders—the Persians, the Greeks, the Romans, the Arabs, the Turks, the French, and the British. All those cultures left fingerprints on the city. Cairo is now a fascinating link between Africa, Arabia, Europe, and Asia. The linkage can be seen in the complexions of the people—ranging from white to brown to black—and in the city's architecture.

Cairo holds more than 15 million people. It is the capital of Egypt and the largest city in Africa. Its residents are called

An artisan at the Cairo Tentmakers' Bazaar sews a beautiful tent panel.

The Cairo Tower at sunset

Above: Girls on the outskirts of Cairo
Left: Feluccas (Egyptian sailboats) on the Nile

Cairenes. More than just the Egyptian capital, it is also the cultural and industrial heart of the nation. By no means is it a sanitized, well-run city. To enjoy Cairo, it is best not to bring a watch. The chaotic pace of the city upsets careful plans. Instead, one must always be prepared for the unexpected. This city delights visitors with surprises.

Cairene (KIGH-REEN)

The Mighty Nile

The Nile begins in central Africa and winds through the deserts of Egypt. The river finally empties into the Mediterranean Sea. It is the longest river on earth. Cairo is situated just below the Nile Delta, where the river splits into several branches. For centuries, the Nile has provided water for the people of the northern desert regions. Even today, about 95 percent of Egypt's population lives near the banks of the Nile.

A FOOT IN TWO

WORLDS

Crowded, busy Cairo is a high-tech city. The roofs of apartment buildings sprout satellite TV dishes. Air-conditioners hum and provide relief from the desert heat. But in the shadow of its modern trappings lies an old way of life that the people refuse to abandon. Cairenes live with one foot in the world of tomorrow and another rooted in the distant past.

THE POPULATION CRUSH

Starting in the 1950s, the Egyptian government channeled much of the nation's money into Cairo. Factories, school buildings, hospitals, and housing units were built. Men and women from the countryside flocked to the capital seeking jobs. Newcomers arrived at the rate of 3,000 per day. The city's population exploded from 2 million in 1960 to almost 15 million in 1990. Few places on earth have ever experienced such a rapid growth in population.

Overcrowding became an annoying but accepted part of life. City buses were so jammed that passengers stood on rear bumpers to catch a ride. People arriving from the country set up mud-brick houses on rooftops. Shantytowns made up of straw huts appeared on the banks of the Nile. Many families moved into cemeteries and built shacks, the living alongside the dead. Some neighborhoods became packed with up to 300,000 people per square mile, about 25 times the average density of New York City.

Cairo schoolgirls on their way home

Pedestrians have a hard time crossing this traffic-choked Cairo street.

Donkeys loaded with goods share Cairo streets with cars, buses, trucks, bicycles, and horse-drawn carts.

The vast majority of the new Cairenes were poor. They took menial jobs such as selling shoelaces on the sidewalk. Children from poor families rushed to open the doors of taxicabs in hopes of a tip. Families picked through garbage heaps, looking for something to sell or something to eat.

The rich and the middle classes crowded into Cairo, too. The capital was the best place in the nation to find a respectable government job. The city's universities attracted students from all over Egypt and the world. Well-to-do people brought cars, which added to the crunch on the streets. In modern Cairo, some 2 million cars, trucks, buses, and motorcycles now lock in snarling traffic jams. In addition to motor vehicles, the streets swarm with bicycles, horse-drawn carts, and donkeys loaded with goods. Pedestrians weave around and in between the slow-moving vehicles.

MAGIC IN THE MARKETS

There is an escape from the hectic city of today. It must be remembered that Cairo has a foot in two worlds. Old neighborhoods that support a magical way of life still thrive in the Egyptian capital. Finding the magic of old takes exploration. It also helps to think back to the time of legend.

A powerful sultan once ordered that each woman he married be killed the morning after the wedding. Despite this grim fate, a beautiful woman named Scheherazade agreed to marry the man. She escaped execution by telling the sultan a story every night. When the story reached its most spellbinding moment, Scheherazade stopped. She said she would continue the story the next day. In this manner, she told one thousand and one stories. By the time she finished, the sultan was in love with her and would not have her executed. Thus was born a fantastic book called *The Arabian Nights* or *A Thousand and One Nights*. From this series of stories sprang

Scheherazade (SHUH-HAIR-UH-ZAHD)

Left: Metalware shops in Cairo

Right: A Cairo perfume maker

A Muslim man at an outdoor market in Cairo

Aladdin and the miracle-working genie who lived in a lamp.

The Arabian Nights is a fantasy written hundreds of years ago. No one is sure who made up the stories. It is generally believed that the author was a Cairene.

A flavor of *The Arabian Nights* still lives in the bewildering tangle of streets, alleys, and markets that make up the old neighborhoods of Cairo.

Follow any one of those streets to reach a market section. Don't expect to find a place where goods are sold neatly under one roof. Cairo does have supermarkets and department stores like those in other large cities of the world. A traditional Egyptian market, however, is far different from stores like those. And it is a lot more fun to shop there.

Khan al-Khalili
(HAHN EL-HAH-LEE-LIH)

Stalls at the Khan al-Khalili, a crowded, busy market in Old Cairo

A market section in an old neighborhood is called a *suq*. Shops in a suq are in buildings strung along the sidewalks. Above the shops are tiny apartments. Many of them house the families of the shop owners. The typical shop is small, about the size of an American bedroom. Doors are kept open to welcome customers inside.

Shops line many Cairo streets, and pedestrians throughout the city carry loads of goods on their heads.

suq (SOOK)

Spices for sale at the Khan al-Khalili

In a suq, thousands of shoppers mill about. Everywhere, shoppers and shop owners argue about prices, usually over a cup of tea. The suq seems to be a tidal wave of confusion. But a definite order prevails. One street is devoted to stores selling toys, while another offers nothing but jewelry. A strong aroma in the air announces a section that sells spices such as saffron and ginger. Shops along one narrow alleyway display nothing but fire extinguishers.

khamsin
(HAHM-SEEN)

An Outdoor City

Cairo shop owners keep their doors wide open during business hours. Auto mechanics, craftspeople, and even cooks and bakers work outside whenever possible. The climate of the city—hot and dry—fosters this outdoor way of life. Temperatures during the summer months often soar to 100 degrees Fahrenheit. In April and May, sandstorms called *khamsin* sometimes cover the city. The sandstorms serve as a reminder that Cairo is in the middle of a desert. Typical of a desert climate, the city's nights can be chilly despite torrid temperatures during the day.

These two women in the Old Cairo market section are carrying great loads of goods on their heads.

In the market sections, men and women carry great loads of goods on their heads. Some stack dozens of bread loaves on a tray the size of a surfboard. With their hands, they balance the tray on their heads and weave through the crowd. Amazingly, they never lose a loaf. Donkeys and donkey carts also bring goods to the markets. When a man leading a donkey wishes to get through a crowded street, he emits a menacing hiss as if he were a snake. Trucks cause the worst disruption in Old Cairo's markets.

Cairo's Camel Market, the largest in all of Africa, is held on Friday mornings.

Truck drivers arrogantly press their vehicles forward and part the crowd like a snowplow.

It is remarkably easy to get lost while visiting a suq in an old neighborhood. Landmarks disappear in the sea of people, animals, and vehicles. Streets twist and bend like rivers. But getting lost is half the fun. A lost shopper will find a surprise around every corner. Being lost and bewildered sparks a person's imagination. Perhaps the lost visitor will feel the spirit of *The Arabian Nights*, and almost hear the words written by that long-ago author: "Her houses are palaces; her air is soft . . . and how can Cairo be otherwise, when she is the Mother of the World?"

THE OTHER WAY OF LIFE

The Cairo Tower is on Gezirah Island.

Gezirah is one of two large islands that nestle in the Nile. The other is Rawdah Island. The islands are part of the modern city. They are connected to the main part of the city by bridges. On Gezirah is a sporting club adorned with grassy fields. One hundred years ago, British army officers amused themselves at the club by playing tennis, golf, and polo. At the time, Egyptian Cairenes were not allowed on the grounds of the sporting club. Today, the club caters to very rich Egyptians as well as to foreigners. About 200,000 millionaires live in Cairo. Many are members of the Gezirah Sporting Club. On club grounds, children of the rich learn how to play tennis. Just a mile away, children of the poor play marbles with stones.

Also on Gezirah Island is Zamalek, Cairo's most fashionable neighborhood. Elegant houses and apartments line Zamalek's tree-shaded streets. Private schools there have classrooms with 20 to 25 students per teacher. In the poorer neighborhoods, the

Gezirah (GAH-ZEE-RAH)
Rawdah (RAOW-THAH)
Zamalek (ZAH-MAH-LIK)

classroom teacher has to cope with 50 or more students. Zamalek is one of the city's few exclusively rich districts. Unlike many other cities, Cairo rarely separates the rich from the poor. Great family houses owned by lawyers or doctors rise next to humble shacks.

Though they often live near one another, the gap between wealthy and impoverished Cairenes seems to grow greater each year. The capital's universities are among the finest in the world. Yet, about one in five adult Cairenes were too poor to attend school when they were young and now cannot read or write. Cairo is a city of great contrasts. Its saddest contrast is the wide gulf between the rich and the poor.

An afternoon stroll on a Cairo street

Egyptian boys with their donkey on the outskirts of Cairo

A CITY OF THE AGES

How old are the Pyramids of Giza? Consider this. Three centuries before the birth of Christ, a Greek traveler named Antipater of Sidon wrote a famous list of all the great structures ever built by human beings. He called the list the "Seven Wonders of the World." Heading the list were the huge Pyramids of Giza near Cairo. They are the only example of the Seven Wonders of the World that still stand today. How ancient are the pyramids? At the time of Antipater, they were more than 2,000 years old.

GRANDEUR OF THE PAST

Long before history was written, men and women gathered in northern Africa. They settled along the Nile to farm soil made fertile by the river. As centuries passed, the Egyptians developed a brilliant society. They were among the first to use writing. They devised a calendar based on a 365-day year. Those early Egyptians were a highly disciplined people whose leaders were called *pharaohs*.

pharaoh (FAY-ROH)
Tutankhamen (TOO-TAHN-KAH-MEHN)

Right: This detail from the throne of Tutankhamen shows the pharaoh, wearing a triple crown, with his wife.

Below: The Nile River

Religion dominated the lives of the ancient Egyptians. To them, death was merely a passage into a new realm. A major function of ancient Egyptian society was to ensure that their pharaohs were comfortable in the life to come. For this reason, the people built pyramids. These were marvelous tombs designed for the pleasure of departed leaders. Pyramids were thought of as stepping-stones to heaven.

Above: An Egyptian wall painting showing a nobleman with his wife and daughter hunting birds along the Nile

This wall relief found in a pyramid shows early Egyptians fishing.

A statue of Pharaoh Rameses IV, 1165 B.C.

After a reign that lasted more than 3,000 years, the Egypt of the pharaohs finally faded. The death blow came from foreign invaders. Among the first of the warriors to sweep over Egypt were the Persians. They conquered the region in 525 B.C. Next came the Greeks under the mighty general Alexander the Great. The Romans followed the Greeks.

The waves of conquerors brought new religions to the land of Egypt. The Romans introduced Christianity.

The Romans conquered Egypt in 30 B.C.

Christian missionaries spoke of a heavenly afterlife. That message had a powerful effect on the Egyptians. After all, their ancestors had built splendid pyramids for their pharoahs as stepping-stones to the afterlife. In the third century A.D., Egyptian Christians formed what is called the Coptic Church. Today, 10 percent of Egyptians are Copts. More than 1 million Coptic Christians live in modern Cairo.

St. George's Church in Old Cairo (right) is a Coptic Christian church.

Muhammad (MOH-HAHM-MAHD)
Islam (IHS-LAHM)

Above: A page from the Koran, the holy book of Islam

The prophet Muhammad (left) is thought of by Muslims as the "seal of the prophet," or the "last messenger of God."

It was the religion of Islam, however, that had the most profound impact on the people of Egypt. Arabs brought Islam to the area in the 600s. Islamic belief centered on the worship of one god (Allah). The religion taught that God's messenger was the prophet Muhammad. He is thought of as the "seal of the prophet," the last messenger of God. The prophet delivered a body of laws and moral codes spelled out in the holy book called the Koran. Today, Islam is the state religion of Egypt. Its prayer schedules and holidays govern the life of Cairo—and nearly all Egyptian communities, big or small.

THE OLD CITY

For more than 5,000 years, cities stood near the site of today's Cairo. But Cairo as we know it was born in relatively recent times. Its birth is connected to an often told story.

In A.D. 969, a Muslim general named Jawhar conquered Egypt. Jawhar ordered hundreds of soldiers to create a rope fence around the sands and ruins where Cairo is now located. The general wished to build a great city to serve as capital of his empire. But first, Jawhar spoke with his astrologers. They told him the planets and stars must be in a perfect position before construction could begin. The astrologers tied bells to the rope fence. When Mars was at its full height, they would ring the bells. Then a small army of workers would start digging the foundations for buildings. However, those careful plans went awry. A raven landed on the rope fence, ringing the bells. The workers started their tasks while Mars was still rising. The astrologers were aghast! This would spell doom for the new city.

Jawhar (JOH-HAHR)

These ancient city gates now enclose the Khan al-Khalili suq area of Old Cairo.

The Suez Canal

The Suez Canal is a 100-mile-long waterway that connects the Mediterranean and the Red Sea. When it was completed in 1869, the canal offered a shortcut for European ships trading with East Asia. It saved both time and money. The French were largely responsible for building the canal, but the British benefited most from the waterway. The canal shortened the route from England to India by about 6,000 miles.

Suez (SOO-EZZ)
El Qahira (EL KAH-HIH-RAH)

This legend told about the founding of Cairo is true in one regard: General Jawhar did indeed build a new capital city at Cairo in the 960s. Jawhar called the city El Qahira. That is an Arabic term meaning "the triumphant" or "the conqueror." Italian merchants later simplified its pronunciation to "Cairo." Was the part about the raven ringing the bells true? Probably not, but the frantic pace of modern Cairo still has a way of disrupting plans. And, of course, the city was not doomed as General Jawhar's astrologers had feared. Instead, Cairo became one of the biggest and most interesting cities on the face of the earth.

THE NEW CITY

In 1798, a French army marched into Cairo. Commanding the troops was Napoleon Bonaparte. This French army commander would soon rule much of Europe. The French easily defeated the Turks, who had occupied the city since 1517. The Turks were the latest of a long line of foreign powers who had dominated Egypt since the time of the pharaohs.

Though they were conquerors, the French had the curiosity of tourists. One of Napoleon's officers who visited the pyramids was awestruck at the sight. He wrote, "Seen from a distance, they produce the same kind of effect as do high mountain peaks. . . . But when you are within a short distance, a wholly different impression is produced. You are struck by surprise. . . .

French army commander Napoleon Bonaparte (left) and his soldiers were awestruck at the sight of the Pyramids of Giza (above).

Finally, when you have reached the foot of the Great Pyramid, you are seized with a vivid and powerful emotion, tempered by a sort of stupefaction, almost overwhelming in its effects."

Although they were impressed by the pyramids, the soldiers might very well have behaved like vandals. It is believed that French gunners blasted the face of the Sphinx with their cannons—just to have "fun." For that reason, the Sphinx now has a large chunk missing from its nose.

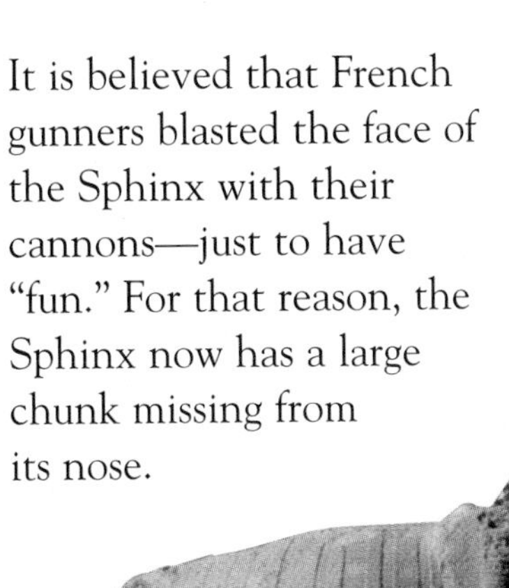

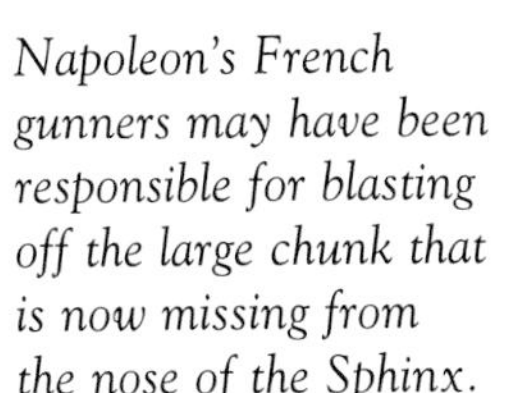

Napoleon's French gunners may have been responsible for blasting off the large chunk that is now missing from the nose of the Sphinx.

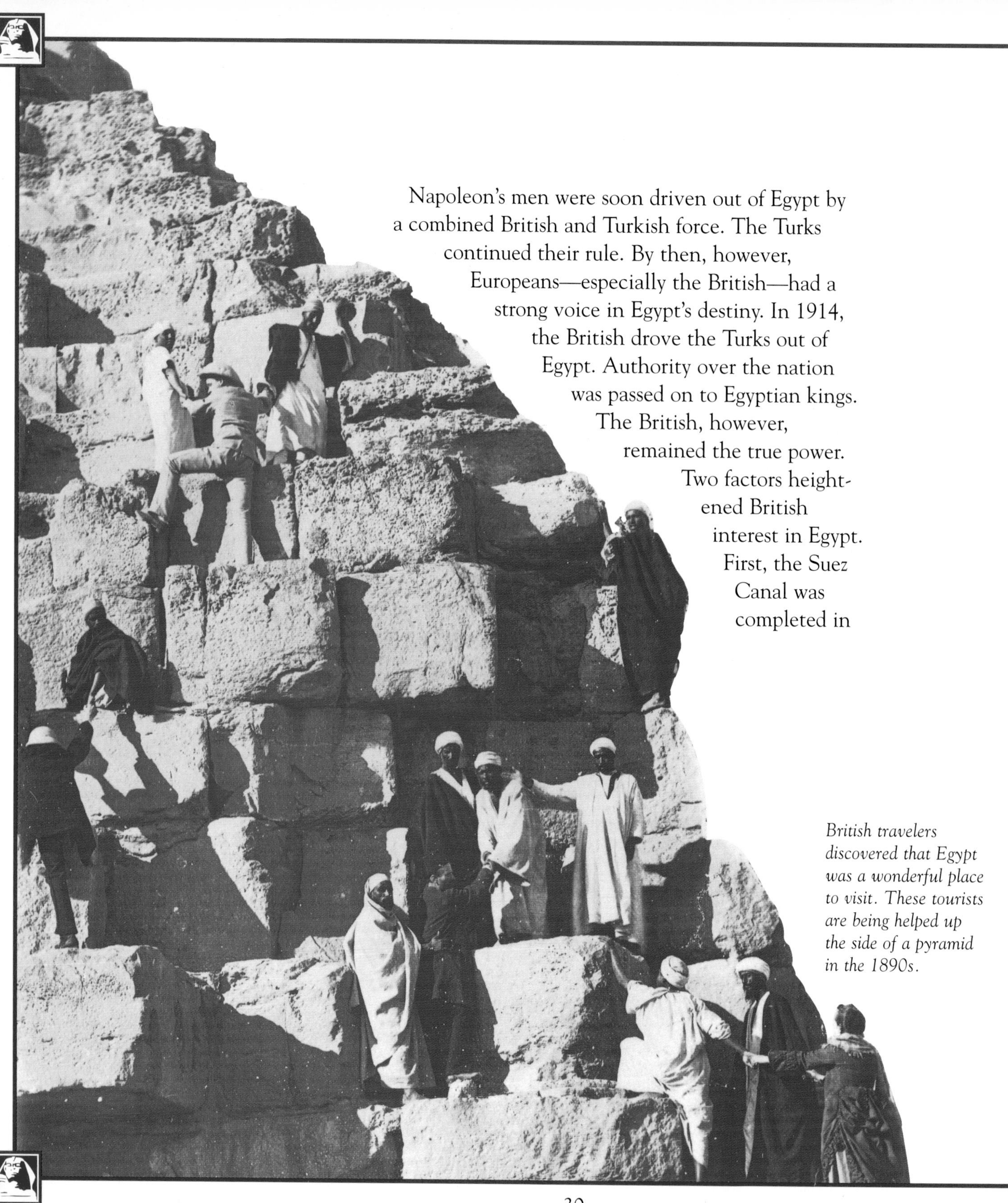

Napoleon's men were soon driven out of Egypt by a combined British and Turkish force. The Turks continued their rule. By then, however, Europeans—especially the British—had a strong voice in Egypt's destiny. In 1914, the British drove the Turks out of Egypt. Authority over the nation was passed on to Egyptian kings. The British, however, remained the true power.

Two factors heightened British interest in Egypt. First, the Suez Canal was completed in

British travelers discovered that Egypt was a wonderful place to visit. These tourists are being helped up the side of a pyramid in the 1890s.

European tourists in Egypt sent postcards like this to their friends and families back home.

Ferdinand de Lesseps raised much of the money that was needed to construct the Suez Canal.

1869. The canal made Egypt a major crossroads in world trade. Second, well-to-do British men and women discovered that Egypt was an exciting place to visit. London couples delighted in showing photographs of themselves standing before the Sphinx. Hoping to make money in trade and tourism, thousands of Europeans poured into Cairo in the 1870s and 1880s. One Egyptian leader complained, "My country is no longer in Africa; we are now part of Europe."

Cook's Tours

Boatloads of tourists came to Cairo via the Suez Canal. The most successful of the tourist companies was owned by Englishman Thomas Cook. He took his first tour group to Cairo in 1869. In the years to come, British families were willing to spend hundreds of pounds to take a "Cook's Tour" to see the fabulous pyramids and the Sphinx.

A scene in the Old City in the early 1900s

The Europeans who arrived in the 1800s demanded luxury hotels, theaters, shops, and an opera house. To meet the demands, European money built a new city alongside the old. New Cairo featured broad, ruler-straight boulevards. The plan of the new city was based on that of Paris. At the time, Paris was undergoing major reconstruction to bring it into the modern age. As construction progressed, two distinct cities emerged side by side. To the east sprawled Egyptian Cairo, the old city with its spiderweb of streets. To the west rose European Cairo, the new city, a place where boulevards intersected in neat, gridlike patterns.

In the early 1900s, the social center of the new city was the Shepheard's Hotel. Founded by Englishman Samuel Shepheard, the hotel catered to wealthy Europeans and Americans. Gourmet meals were served in the hotel's dining room. Men wearing spotless white suits sipped drinks at its bar. Rarely did Egyptians venture into the Shepheard's Hotel except to work as cooks and dishwashers. In fact, poor Egyptians shunned the new city altogether. To them, European Cairo was a strange and hostile place—even though it lay alongside the old city.

Foreign domination finally came to an end in 1952. In that year, a group of army officers led by Gamal Abdel Nasser seized Egypt. To celebrate Nasser's uprising, mobs burned down the Shepheard's Hotel. Though property was destroyed, the revolution was bloodless. All over Cairo, people rejoiced. For the first time since the pharaohs—twenty-five centuries in the past—Egypt was led by Egyptians.

Before it was burned down in 1952, the Shepheard's Hotel catered to European tourists.

"The [neighborhood] was very congested. Already teeming with more than its normal pedestrian traffic, it was being flooded by currents of human beings from Al-Ataba. The April sun cast fiery rays [as the two men] made their way through the throngs." These lines begin a chapter in the novel *Sugar Street*, written by Naguib Mahfouz. Mahfouz writes stories about the problems and joys of Cairo's families. He is the city's most beloved writer.

Al-Ataba (EL-AH-TAH-BAH)
Naguib Mahfouz (NAH-GEEB MAH-FOOZ)

ISLAM, THE SOUL OF THE CITY

Just a glance at Cairo's skyline shows dozens of tall narrow towers called *minarets*. The minarets rise above *mosques* (Islamic houses of worship). Five times a day—at dawn, at noon, in the afternoon, in the evening, and at nightfall—a crier climbs to the top of a minaret and calls people to prayer. Public prayer is an ancient requirement of the Islamic religion. In modern Cairo the crier, called a *muezzin*, will often announce his message over a loudspeaker. It is the only way he can be heard above the clamor of city traffic.

The practice of Islam rules Cairo's daily life. At prayer time, even the city's TV shows

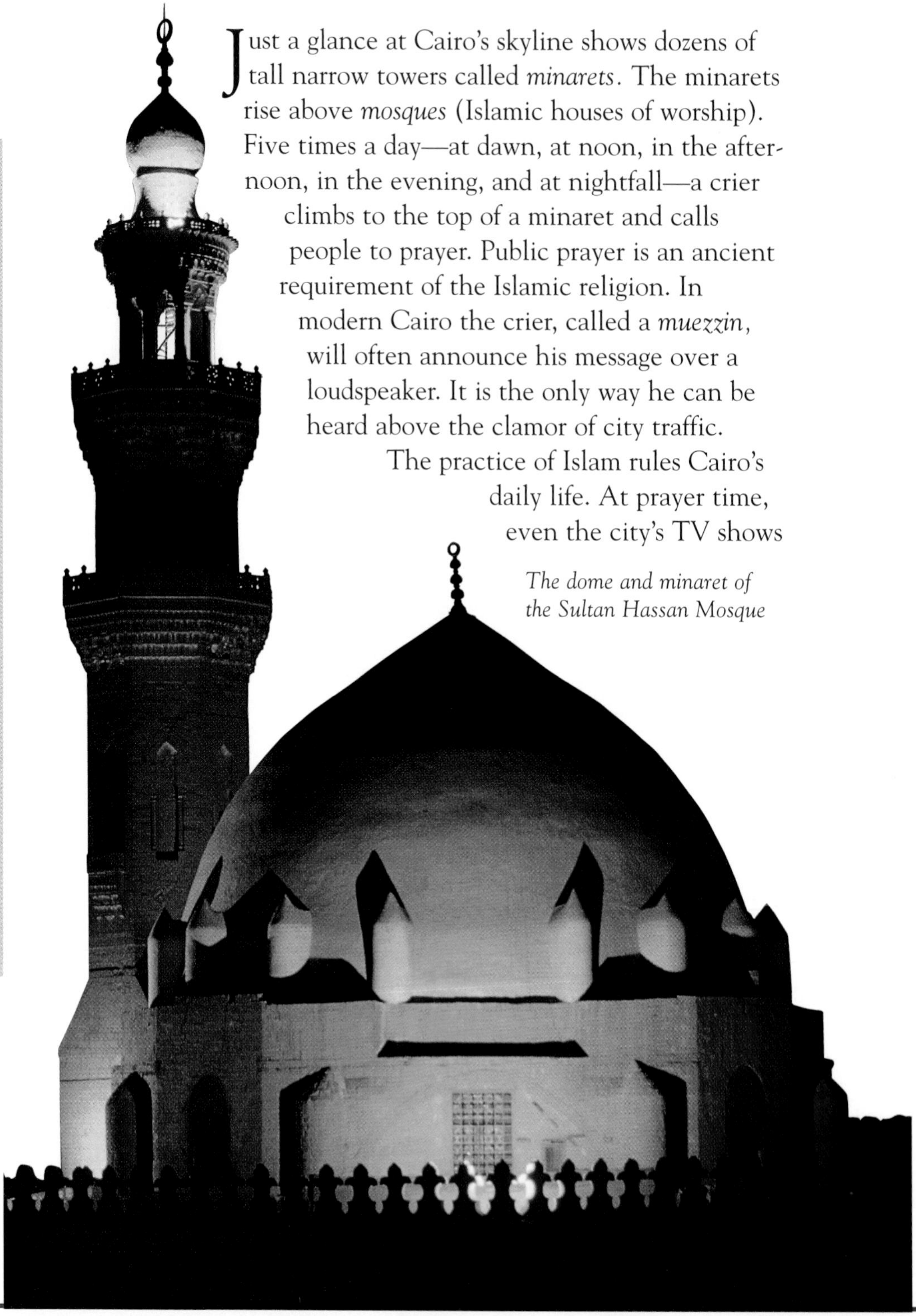

The dome and minaret of the Sultan Hassan Mosque

Naguib Mahfouz

Born in Cairo in 1911, Naguib Mahfouz has a deep understanding of life in the city. His best-known work is the *Cairo Trilogy*, three books that trace the fortunes and misfortunes of a Cairo family. For many years, Mahfouz's books were read only in Egypt. Then, in 1988, Mahfouz won the Nobel Prize for literature. His books are now loved by people throughout the world.

minaret (MIHN-AH-RET)
mosque (MOSK)
muezzin (MOO-AH-ZIHN)

The Sultan Hassan Mosque

fade out to remind people to worship. Islamic laws forbid lying, stealing, or committing murder. Largely because of these laws, people who walk the streets of Cairo feel safe. In the markets, goods are displayed on open counters. Thieves or shoplifters are rare. Any thief who is caught is dealt with severely.

Friday prayers at Al-Hussein Mosque

Islam is celebrated in everyday artworks enjoyed by the people. Carpets made in Cairo have intricate designs. Those designs stem from the days when Islamic artists were not allowed to depict living figures. It was feared that such figures might be worshiped as false gods.

It is the duty of every Islamic person to journey to the holy city of Mecca (in Saudi Arabia) at least once in a lifetime. Such a pilgrimage is called a *hajj*. Upon returning from Mecca, many Cairenes hire neighborhood artists to paint highlights of their hajj on the front of their houses. In the old days, such paintings showed a camel train. Today, hajj drawings may include a picture of a jet plane.

A follower of Islam is called a Muslim, meaning one who submits to God. Cairo's Muslims observe many feasts and festivals. None is more important than

An Egyptian hand-woven silk carpet

More than a million Muslims make pilgrimages to Mecca, Saudi Arabia, each year. Huge crowds gather to pray in the courtyard of the Great Mosque.

hajj (HODGE)
Muslim (MOOS-LIHM)

Many Muslims hire artists to paint hajj scenes on the front of their houses.

Ramaden (RAH-MAH-<u>TH</u>AN)
iftar (IF-TAHR)

Ramadan. This is a month-long period of fasting. It honors the time when God sent the holy Koran to the prophet Muhammad. For thirty days, Muslims refuse food and drink during the daylight hours. Daylight is defined to be, "as long as a white thread can be distinguished from a black thread." Ramadan can fall in the summer months, when daylight lingers in Cairo for sixteen hours. Refraining from all liquids under the city's scorching sun is an ordeal. When night finally comes, families quench their thirst and eagerly dig into their evening meal, the *iftar.*

At the end of Ramadan, the city explodes with celebration. People hug each other in the streets. Boys set off firecrackers. The devout have completed their fast. Now is the time for laughter.

Muslim Cairenes

WOMEN AND ISLAM

Cairo men enjoy smoking tobacco, drinking coffee, and chatting in the city's coffeehouses.

Coffeehouses are popular gathering places in Cairo. Customers sit at tables, chatting and drinking strong coffee sweetened with sugar. Some smoke tobacco through water pipes. Everyone seems at ease. But if a woman should accidentally walk through the door, conversation stops. The men stare at her. Usually, the embarrassed woman leaves. No law says that a woman cannot go to a coffeehouse. In fact, some coffeehouses welcome customers who are women. However, at least nine out of ten such establishments will chase a woman away with curious looks.

Islamic customs spell out vastly different roles for men and for women. Respect for women is demanded by the Koran. Assaulting a woman is an almost unforgivable sin. Still, many Muslim men—and some women—believe in an old adage: "A woman should be ruled by her father until she is married, her husband after marriage."

Cairo has long been considered a progressive place in the Islamic world. Today, more than one-third of the city's university

This Muslim woman probably would not feel welcome at a coffeehouse.

ost Muslim women, like those wn at right and below, wear a head covering called a higab.

students are female. Women serve as doctors, lawyers, and government officials. Yet restrictions on women still linger. The restrictions are unwritten and often unsaid. They baffle foreigners—and even confuse Cairenes.

The way a woman is expected to dress is one of many confusing restrictions. When going to work, most women wear a *higab*, a head covering. Women also cover their necks and their arms. Islam dictates that a woman's clothes should conceal her body. Even those Cairene women who do not wear a head covering still dress conservatively.

higab (HIH-GAHB)
Umm Kulthum (OMM KAHL-THOOM)

Umm Kulthum (1898-1975)

The men in the coffeehouses, especially the older ones, often discuss a legendary woman singer named Umm Kulthum. Born into a poor family, she began singing at weddings. Her golden voice made her the rage of Cairo. She was also popular in other Arab countries. Some say she did more to promote Arab unity than did any political leader. Umm Kulthum died in 1975. Her funeral was held in Cairo. Thousands of the city's men and women lined the streets waving handkerchiefs, weeping, and singing her love songs.

GROWING UP IN CAIRO

Though the city is ancient, its people are young. About half the population of Cairo is under the age of eighteen. What do children do in this densely populated and largely impoverished city? They do what children everywhere do. They go to school, and they play games when they are not in school.

Hopscotch is a favorite game among the girls of Cairo. When playing on the sidewalk, girls draw the hopscotch grid in chalk. In the empty lots, they use a stick to mark the lines on sand. Boys rarely play hopscotch. Instead, boys are devoted to soccer. Soccer games rage in the parks and on side streets.

Impoverished boys cannot afford to buy a soccer ball. No problem. They make a ball by stuffing rags into an old sock. Poverty also prevents many children from buying marbles. Again this poses no problem. Poor children play a game called *seegha*. The same rules apply in seegha, but the children use pebbles instead of marbles.

seegha (SEE-GHAH)

These Cairene boys enjoy playing soccer when they are not in school.

Egyptian law says that all children between the ages of six and fifteen must go to school. Not many years ago, poor children rarely went to classes. For this reason, a large percentage of adult Cairenes today cannot read or write. School attendance is now required, and schools have tough standards. Students progress through six years of primary school, three years of middle school, and three years of high school. They must pass a very demanding exam to go from one stage to the next. On exam day, parents wait outside the school and anxiously ask their sons and daughters how they did on the test. The most dreaded exam comes after a student completes high school and wishes to attend the university. Many students emerge from that test in tears.

The parents of the Cairo schoolchildren shown on this page may not be able to read and write.

Most boys and girls in Cairo wear uniforms to school. They rise together when the teacher enters the room. Students are also expected to stand up when addressing the teacher individually. Religion is a required course. Muslim children study the Koran, while Christians read the Bible. During lunchtime, the rules are relaxed. In Egypt, it is not considered polite to eat in front of another person without offering to share the food. Therefore, children freely exchange sandwiches and fruit during lunch period. And, of course, they chat and giggle. Sometimes the din in a lunchroom is overwhelming.

A traveling market awaits students at dismissal time. Impoverished Cairenes sell goods to children to earn a few pennies. So, at three o'clock, a small army of pushcart salesmen descends on the school gates.

A Cairo schoolgirl in uniform

A cart with a chimney on top sells steamed sweet potatoes. Other vendors sell sunflower seeds wrapped in paper cones. One cart is loaded with mulberry leaves and stacks of shoeboxes. The owner of this cart sells the *dood el-azz,* a silkworm. Inside each box is a delicate silkworm nibbling on leaves. A child will buy a box, take it home, and observe the worm's progress through a peephole. As the weeks go by, the worm transforms into a cocoon and finally into a moth. Then the child lets it fly free. As a moth, the worm has achieved adulthood. So will the child, some day.

dood el-azz
(DOOD EL-AZZ)

Girls buying steamed sweet potatoes from a vendor

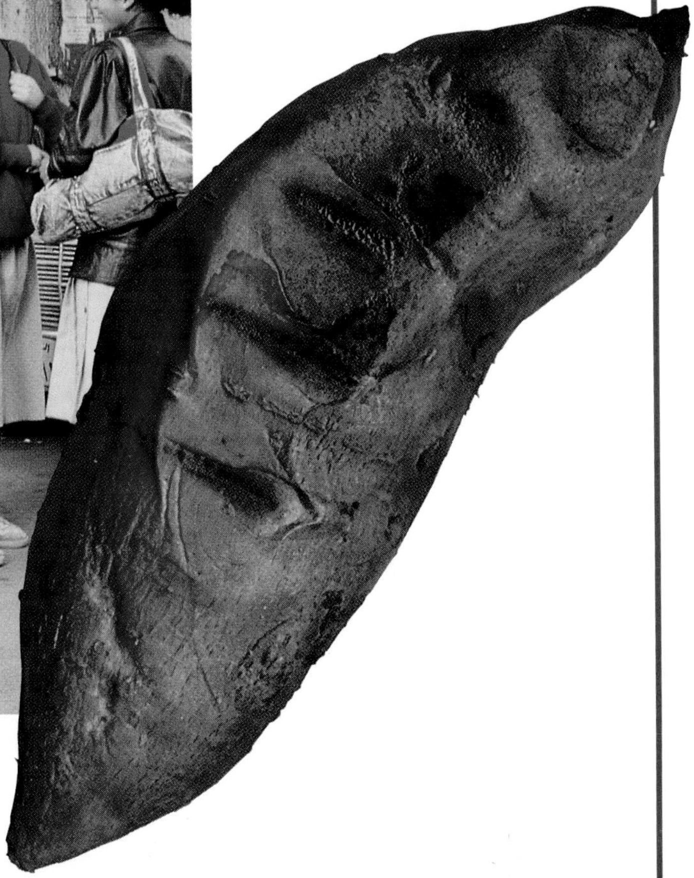

Every day, tour buses packed with visitors from around the world push through Cairo's crowded streets. Tour boats with glass tops motor down the Nile. Inside the boats and buses, guides point out Cairo's highlights. There are so many amazing things to see that visitors should be prepared for a busy trip.

GIFTS OF THE PHARAOHS

Most visitors make the pyramids their first stop. There are more than 80 pyramids in Egypt. The largest and best preserved are the three Pyramids of Giza. They rise on the outskirts of Cairo. It is believed that the Giza pyramids were built between 2600 and 2500 B.C. The biggest of the three is called Cheops. It was named for the pharaoh who was buried there. It is also known as the Great Pyramid. The Great Pyramid contains more than 2 million stone blocks. Each block weighs about 2.5 tons. The ancient builders used no mortar or plaster to join the blocks together. Yet each block was cut so precisely that, even today, a sharp knife cannot be squeezed into the seams. Modern construction experts shake their heads in wonder when they

Cheops (KEE-OPS)

The Great Pyramid of Cheops at Giza

The Sphinx

consider the enormity of the pyramid-building task.

Visitors may tour the inside of the Great Pyramid. They enter a narrow corridor and emerge into the king's chamber. It is believed that the pharaoh was once laid to rest in this room. A tangle of lesser corridors awaits the bold tourist. Walking in the narrow hallways is not for anyone who panics when forced to squeeze through tight spaces. The pharaohs may have built these massive tombs to discourage grave robbers. But grave robbers still found ways to steal the gold and other objects the pharaohs expected to enjoy in the afterlife. No treasure has ever been found in the Pyramids of Giza.

The mysterious Sphinx lies almost in the shadow of the Great

The interior of the Great Pyramid of Cheops at Giza

Pyramid. With its body shaped like that of a lion, it is thought that the Sphinx was built to protect the pyramid complex. The face of the Sphinx is carved from solid rock. Sadly, air pollution drifting in from Cairo is eating away at the Sphinx. Experts worry that the Sphinx—a survivor for almost 5,000 years—may soon become disfigured by Cairo's foul air.

MUSEUMS—PRESERVING THE PAST

After Giza, the city's second most popular tourist stop is the Egyptian Museum. The elegant museum building was completed in 1902. It contains the world's largest collection of Egyptian antiquities. The most popular exhibit there is the Treasures of Tutankhamen. "King Tut," as he is often called, was a handsome young man when he died in 1324 B.C. His tomb was not discovered until 1922. Amazingly, it was untouched by grave robbers. Items such as the king's bows and arrows were taken from the tomb and are now displayed at the Egyptian Museum. Most spectacular of all is Tutankhamen's death mask. The mask is solid gold and a masterpiece of ancient craftsmanship.

The Museum of Islamic Art contains more than 75,000 objects. On display are beautiful handwritten books, metal water jugs shaped like birds or animals, and splendid woodcarvings. The Coptic Museum celebrates Cairo's Christians. The museum holds objects found in Christian monasteries that stood in Egypt before the coming of Islam in the 600s.

The Art and Life Center is a museum set in a handsome house once owned by a member of Egypt's royal family. The center displays Egyptian art from ancient

The beautiful solid-gold death mask of King Tutankhamen (left) is on display in the Egyptian Museum (below).

This mummified dog is on display in the National Museum of Egypt.

papyrus
(PUH-PIGH-RUS)
Pharoanic
(FEH-RAY-AH-NIK)

The Cairo Metro

Going from museum to museum can be difficult if you take a taxi. Taxis get mired in traffic jams. A more efficient way to get around is by using the Metro, the city's recently opened subway. Clean and speedy, the Metro was built with the help of French engineers. Its only problem is its popularity. Millions of passengers use the system each day, and the cars become woefully overcrowded.

to modern times. At the Papyrus Museum, visitors learn how Egyptians made writing paper from papyrus plants. Interestingly, the museum's founder had to import papyrus from the interior of Africa because the plant no longer grows in Egypt. Papyrus used to grow wild along the banks of the Nile.

The Pharaonic Village lies on an island in the Nile just south of Cairo. At the village, actors demonstrate how people in ancient times farmed, created crafts, and sold goods.

At the Pharaonic Village (right), actors show visitors how the ancient Egyptians lived and worked..

GIFTS OF ISLAM

More than 250 mosques stand in the old quarters of eastern Cairo. The mosques are packed so closely together that their minarets look like a stone forest. They are democratic places of worship. Millionaires—and even the president of Egypt—pray side-by-side with beggars.

Muhammad Ali (MOE-HAHM-MAD AH-LEE)
Al-Azhar (EL AZZ-HAR)

The Citadel is a fortress. A mosque stands within its compound. Built in the 1100s, the fort has never been conquered. Not even the Christian Crusaders were able to penetrate its walls. The original walls were made from stones taken from smaller pyramids that once stood at Giza. On the grounds is the striking Muhammad Ali Mosque, which was built in the early 1800s. The Muhammad Ali Mosque features narrow minarets, typical of the Turkish style. The Citadel and its enclosed mosque are among Cairo's most famous landmarks.

Al-Azhar is a university as well as a place of worship. For more than 1,000

The Muhammad Ali Mosque was built in the early 1800s.

The Sultan Hassan Mosque is the largest mosque in Cairo.

years, the university at Al-Azhar has trained Islamic scholars. Today, some 90,000 students from around the world study there. Courses cover all subjects, from medicine to law. The mosque of Al-Azhar has been rebuilt many times over the centuries. It still fulfills one of its original functions by housing needy Muslims making a pilgrimage to Mecca. Al-Azhar means "The Resplendent."

A mosque stands within the compound of the Citadel (left).

The largest mosque in Cairo is the Sultan Hassan. It was built in 1356 in the shape of a cross. Art experts hail the Sultan Hassan Mosque as one of the finest examples of Islamic architecture found anywhere in the world. Its entrance is as tall as a four-story building, and its minarets are the loftiest in Cairo.

Sultan Hassan
(SOHL-TAHN HAS-SAHN)

OTHER TREASURES

On the southern tip of Rawdah Island stands the remains of a Nilometer. This is a device used to measure the rise and fall of the Nile's waters. The Nilometer seen today was built in the year 861. It replaced a Nilometer constructed 150 years before that. A still earlier Nilometer was built by the Romans, and an older one yet was erected on that spot by the pharaohs.

The Manyal Palace on Rawdah Island provides an intriguing look into how Egyptian royalty lived not too many years ago. Work began on the palace in 1901. It took 30 years to complete construction. The inside walls are covered with intricate carvings and mosaics. The long and narrow throne room has a white marble floor. Loveliest of the palace buildings is its mosque, which features stained-glass windows.

Many tourists venture into one of Cairo's Cities of the Dead to enjoy a fascinating side trip. These are cemeteries, but don't

This young girl is a resident of one of Cairo's Cities of the Dead (far right).

expect to see gravestones on a grassy field. Cairo's Cities of the Dead consist of solidly built tombs. The tombs are constructed along an orderly network of streets. In recent years, these cemeteries have been invaded by homeless people. The homeless have built shacks and even grocery stores and restaurants amid the tombs. Travelers entering Cairo 500 years ago wrote that they saw families living in the cemeteries. In today's densely packed city, an estimated 1 million squatters live in the Cities of the Dead.

On Gezirah Island rises the Cairo Tower, a fitting place to begin or end a tour of the city. From the top floor, visitors see buildings as modern as tomorrow and pyramids older than history. This is Cairo, an exciting city whose heart embraces the past and the future.

Manyal (MEHN-YEHL)

The Cairo Tower at sunset

This man is one of about a million people who make their homes in Cairo's Cities of the Dead.

FAMOUS LANDMARKS

A view of Cairo

The Pyramids of Giza

Giza
Located about 9 miles southwest of the city are the three Pyramids of Giza and the Sphinx. Largest of the pyramids is Cheops, which is also called the Great Pyramid. The Pyramids of Giza are the only remaining examples of the Seven Wonders of the World.

The Citadel
One of Cairo's most famous landmarks, the Citadel is a fort with a mosque within its walls. The fort dates back to the 1100s. The enclosed Muhammad Ali Mosque was built in the 1800s.

Sultan Hassan Mosque
The largest mosque in Cairo, the Sultan Hassan was built in 1356. Experts consider it to be a masterpiece of Islamic art.

Al-Azhar
More than 1,000 years old, this compound serves as a university and a mosque. Throughout its long history, the university has trained Islamic scholars. The mosque contains more than 250,000 ancient handwritten manuscripts.

Al-Hakim Mosque
This mosque has had an odd history. It was used as a prison for captured Crusaders. It was destroyed by an earthquake in 1303 and later rebuilt. Napoleon's troops kept horses within its walls. By 1979, it had fallen into ruin. Neighborhood boys used its grounds as a soccer field. Then it was restored, largely by volunteer labor. Today, it stands as one of the city's proud places of worship.

El Aqsunqur
Known as the Blue Mosque, this handsome building has blue-green tiles on one of its walls. The mosque was built in the fourteenth century by Emir Aqsunqur.

Khan al-Khalili
This is the most famous suq in the old section. Foreign tourists gather here to look for bargains in jewelry. Shopkeepers invite tourists inside for a glass of mint tea while they look at items.

Professors entering the interior court of the Al-Azhar university-mosque complex

The Papyrus Museum, located on a houseboat in the Nile

The Egyptian Museum

Abdin Palace

Completed in 1874, this one-time house of royalty is now a government office building. Though not open to tourists, the outside of the building alone gives one an appreciation of the lifestyle of the kings and queens of old Egypt.

Egyptian Museum

The museum contains the world's greatest collection of Egyptian antiquities. Particularly popular is the Tutankhamen Gallery. Here, the treasures of King Tutankhamen (who died in 1324 B.C.) are displayed.

The Coptic Museum

Interesting objects of Cairo's Christian community are presented here.

Bab al-Futuh (Gate of Conquest) and Bab al-Nasr (Gate of Victory)

At one time, these were the gates of Cairo, the main entrance to the walled city. Portions of the old city walls can be seen here.

The Papyrus Museum

Visitors to this museum learn how the ancients made fine paper from the papyrus plant.

Anderson House

This splendid house, graced with period furniture, is open to the public for touring. It was once the private home of British Major Gayer-Anderson. Visitors learn how the foreign community lived in Cairo during the early 1900s.

Gezirah Sporting Club

These grassy fields were once a playground for very wealthy British subjects. It is now a haven for wealthy Egyptians. Some British customs remain, however. Tea and crumpets are still popular in the clubhouse.

The Cairo Tower

Soaring 590 feet in the air, the tower is the city's tallest building. Many Cairenes consider the ultramodern building to be an eyesore, but its top deck offers a striking view of the city.

FAST FACTS

POPULATION

City: 11,155,000
Metropolitan Area: More than 15,000,000
Cairo is the largest city in Africa.

AREA 83 square miles

NEIGHBORHOODS The Nile River runs through the middle of Cairo. It divides the city in many ways. Cairo is a blend of the old and the new. Old neighborhoods lie on the east side of the river. Beginning in the late 1800s, a new European-type city was built on the western bank of the Nile. The newer city features broad streets, parks, and public squares. In the old city are narrow, twisting streets and fascinating market sections called suqs.

CLIMATE Cairo is situated in a desert, and desert weather prevails. Daytime temperatures are hot. Nights can be chilly, even during the summer. Great clouds of sand sometimes blow in from the deserts outside of town. Cairo receives only 1 inch of rainfall a year. The average July high temperature is 96 degrees Fahrenheit; the average low is 70 degrees Fahrenheit; the average January high temperature is 65 degrees Fahrenheit, with a low of 47 degrees Fahrenheit.

INDUSTRIES More than just the political capital of Egypt, Cairo is also the nation's social, cultural, and economic hub. Egypt's movie industry is located in the capital, as are the TV networks and all the major national newspapers. Factories in the metropolitan area produce paper, chemicals, textiles, and food products. Artisans in small shops create jewelry and handicrafts. Tourism is a prime industry. Tourists from all over the world flock to Cairo to see the pyramids and other sights.

CHRONOLOGY

5000 B.C.
Farming communities develop along the Nile.

2600-2500 B.C.
The three great Pyramids of Giza and the Sphinx are completed.

525 B.C.
Persians conquer Egypt, ending the rule of the pharaohs and beginning a long period of foreign domination.

332 B.C.
The Greeks under Alexander the Great defeat the Persians and occupy Egypt.

30 B.C.
The Romans incorporate Egypt into the Roman Empire.

A.D. 600s
Islamic armies occupy Egypt, bringing with them the Islamic religion.

969
Muslim General Jawhar, Egypt's most recent conqueror, founds modern Cairo.

1175
Construction begins on the Citadel, which is now a famous city landmark.

1517
Turkish troops conquer Egypt.

1798
French soldiers under Napoleon enter Cairo.

1801
The French are driven out of Egypt by combined Turkish and British forces.

An Egyptian boy riding a donkey, a common form of transportation in Cairo

1859-1869
The Suez Canal is built, making Cairo a headquarters of world trade.

1914
Britain wages war on Turkey and extends British influence in Egypt.

1927
Cairo's population reaches 1 million.

1952
Gamal Abdel Nasser leads a revolution against the British; for the first time since the pharaohs, Egypt is ruled by Egyptians.

1970
Aswan Dam is completed, ending the annual flooding of the Nile.

1987
The Cairo Metro, Egypt's first subway, is opened for service.

1992
An earthquake strikes Cairo and its suburbs in October, causing more than 560 deaths.

1994
Overcrowded Cairo hosts the World Population Conference; Pope John Paul II is guest speaker.

CAIRO

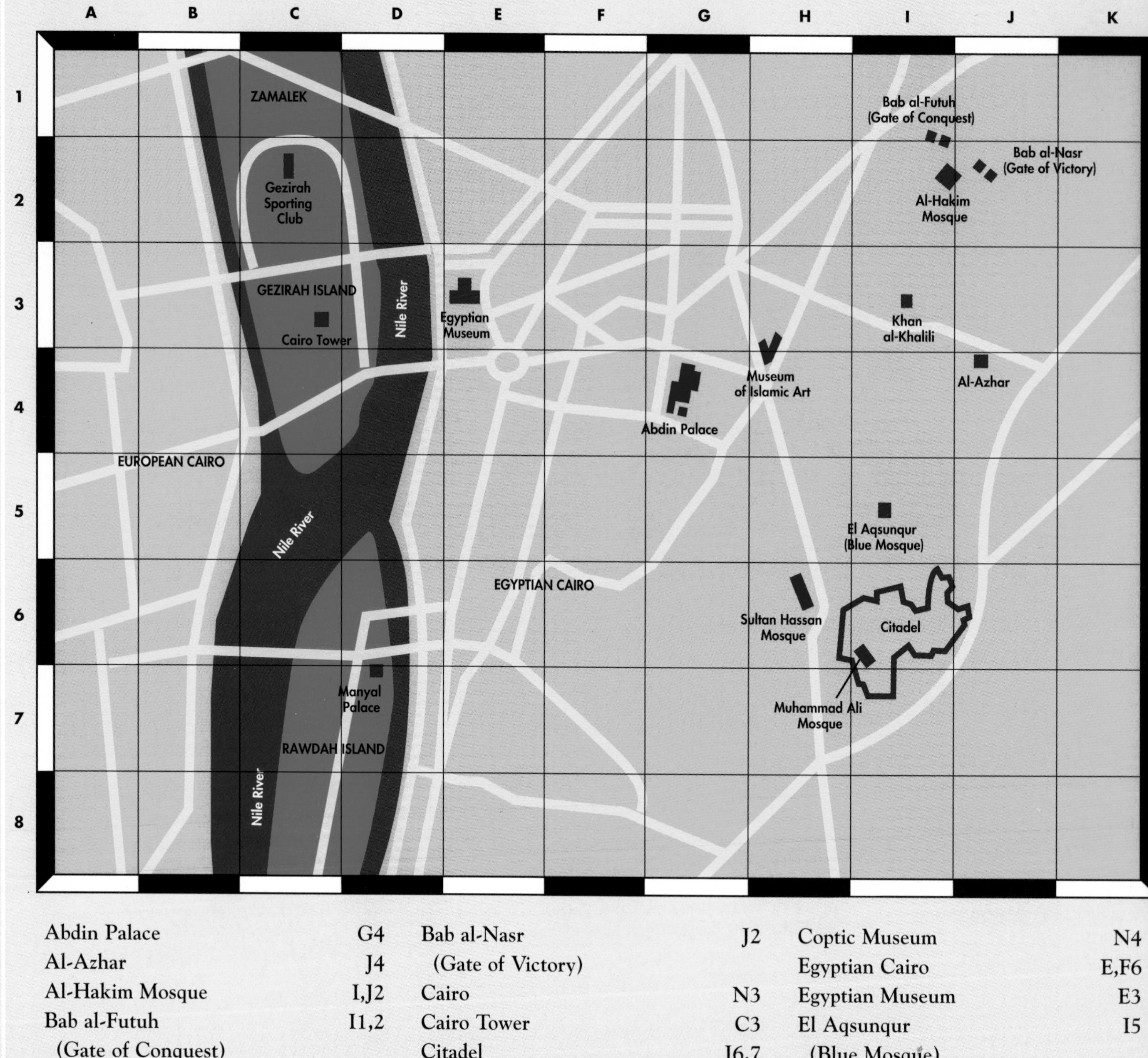

Abdin Palace	G4	Bab al-Nasr (Gate of Victory)	J2	Coptic Museum	N4
Al-Azhar	J4	Cairo	N3	Egyptian Cairo	E,F6
Al-Hakim Mosque	I,J2	Cairo Tower	C3	Egyptian Museum	E3
Bab al-Futuh (Gate of Conquest)	I1,2	Citadel	I6,7	El Aqsunqur (Blue Mosque)	I5

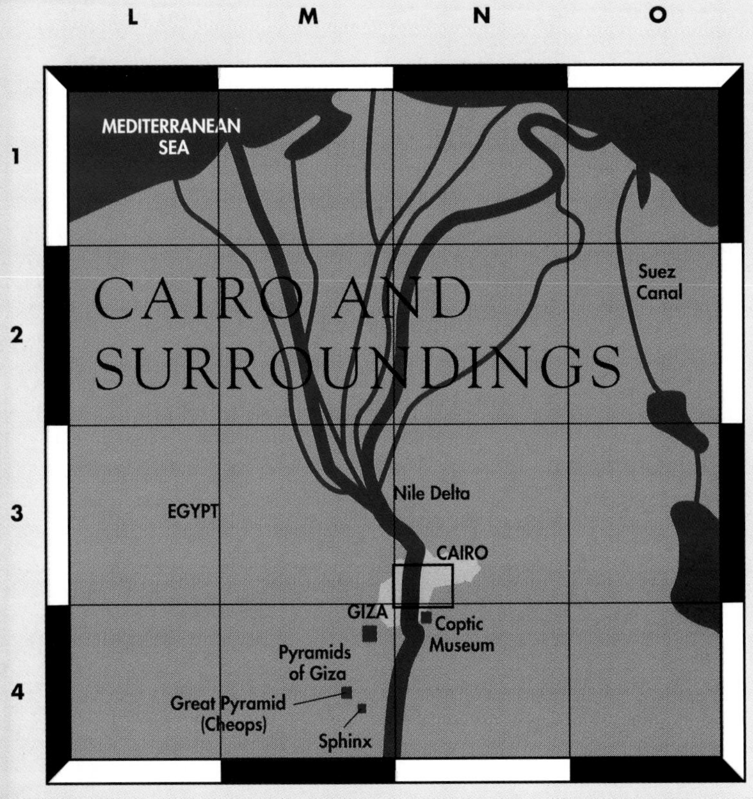

Place	Grid
European Cairo	A,B5
Gezirah Island	C3
Gezirah Sporting Club	C2
Giza	M4
Great Pyramid (Cheops)	M4
Khan al-Khalili	I3
Manyal Palace	D7
Muhammad Ali Mosque	I6
Museum of Islamic Art	H3,4
Nile Delta	M,N,O 1,2,3
Nile River	B,C,D1,2,3,4,5,6,7,8; M,N,O1,2,3,4
Pyramids of Giza	M4
Rawdah Island	C,D 7
Sphinx	M4
Suez Canal	O 1,2
Sultan Hassan Mosque	H6
Zamalek	C1

GLOSSARY

adage: An old saying or bit of wisdom

aghast: Shocked, repulsed

arrogantly: In a superior manner, without regard for the feelings of others

astrologer: A person who forecasts the future by studying the passage of the stars and planets

awry: Not according to plan

chaotic: Confused and unorganized

cope: To put up with or endure

devise: To invent or create

devout: Sincere in one's religious beliefs

din: Noise or racket

disruption: Sudden interruption

dominate: To control

gourmet restaurant: A restaurant that caters to people who appreciate exellent food

high-tech: High-technology; modern

intricate: Complicated; interwoven

menial: Requiring little skill or education

mosaic: Picture or design made by placing colored tiles on plaster

pilgrimage: Journey made for religious reasons

readily: Easily, willingly

site: Place or location

squatter: A person who moves onto unoccupied land and pays no rent to stay there

stupefaction: Amazement, astonishment

sultan: Ruler of an Islamic country

torrid: Extremely hot

Picture Identifications

Cover: A reproduction of a tomb painting at Pharaonic Village, the death mask of King Tutankhamen, a downtown view of Cairo, girls with goods from the market
Page 1: Egyptian men
Pages 4-5: The Sphinx and one of the Pyramids of Giza
Pages 8-9: A vegetable stall in a market section of Cairo
Pages 20-21: The Pyramids of Giza
Pages 34-35: A group of Islamic Cairenes resting and chatting
Pages 46-47: A felucca on the Nile sails past the Cairo Tower

Photo Credits:

Cover (top left), ©**Richard Nowitz;** cover (top right), ©**SuperStock International, Inc.;** cover (bottom right), ©Kathleen Campbell/**Tony Stone Images, Inc.;** cover (background), ©Will & Deni McIntyre/**Tony Stone Images, Inc.;** 1, ©Jean Higgins/Unicorn Stock Photos; 3, ©KK&A, Ltd; 4-5, ©Prim and Ray Manley/**SuperStock International, Inc.;** 6 (both pictures), ©**Richard Nowitz;** 7 (top left), ©W. Otto/**H. Armstrong Roberts;** 7 (top right), ©R.T. Nowitz/**Photo Researchers, Inc.;** 7 (bottom), ©**Photri, Inc.;** 8-9, ©Charlie Waite/**Tony Stone Images, Inc.;** 10 (left), ©**Robert Holmes;** 10 (right), ©**Diana Rasche;** 11 (left), ©Jean Higgins/**Unicorn Stock Photos;** 11 (shoelaces), ©**KK&A, Ltd.;** 12 (left), ©Marc A. Auth/**N E Stock Photo;** 12 (right), ©Donna Carroll/**Travel Stock;** 13 (top), ©Bachmann/**N E Stock Photo;** 13 (bottom), ©Ben Edwards/**Tony Stone Images, Inc.;** 14 (left), ©Jean Higgins/**Unicorn Stock Photos;** 14 (right), ©DAMM/ZEFA/**H. Armstrong Roberts;** 15 (top), ©Larry Tackett/**Tom Stack & Assoc.;** 15 (necklace), ©**KK&A, Ltd.;** 15 (bottom right), ©Marilyn Kazmers-SharkSong/**Dembinsky Photo Assoc.;** 16 (left), ©Donna Carroll/**Travel Stock;** 16 (right), ©**Donna Rasche;** 17 (both pictures), ©**Richard Nowitz;** 18 (top), ©**Photri, Inc.;** 18 (tennis balls), ©**KK&A, Ltd.;** 19 (top), ©**Richard T. Nowitz;** 19 (bottom), ©Marilyn Kazmers-SharkSong/**Dembinsky Photo Assoc.;** 20-21, ©**R.T. Nowitz;** 22 (top), ©Fred Maroon/**Photo Researchers, Inc.;** 22 (bottom), ©DAMM/ZEFA/**H. Armstrong Roberts;** 23 (top & bottom right), British Museum/**e.t. archive;** 23 (bottom left), ©Marilyn Kazmers-SharkSong/**Dembinsky Photo Assoc.**; 24 (left), **Bettmann;** 24 (right), ©**R.T. Nowitz;** 25 (left), **Mary Evans Picture Library;** 25 (right), private collection/**e.t. archive;** 26-27 (rope & bells), ©**KK&A, Ltd.**; 26 (right), ©**Photri, Inc.;** 27 (top), **Mary Evans Picture Library;** 28 (left), **Mary Evans Picture Library;** 28 (right), ©Doug Armand/**Tony Stone Images, Inc.;** 29, ©Doug Armand/**Tony Stone Images, Inc.;** 30, **Corbis-Bettmann;** 31 (left), Musee Bonnat Bayonne/**e.t. archive;** 31 (right), **Mary Evans Picture Library;** 32 (top), ©Werner Otto/**Tony Stone Images, Inc.;** 32 (bottom), ©**Archive Photos;** 33, **Corbis-Bettmann;** 34-35, ©**Robert Holmes;** 36, ©**Richart T. Nowitz;** 37 (top), ©Margot Granitsas/**Photo Researchers, Inc.;** 37 (bottom), ©**Robert Holmes;** 38 (top), ©C. Osborne/**Photo Researchers, Inc.;** 38 (bottom), ©M. Biber/**Photo Researchers, Inc.;** 39 (top), ©**Diana Rasche;** 39 (bottom), ©Jean Higgins/**Unicorn Stock Photos;** 40 (left), ©Sarah Stone/**Tony Stone Images, Inc.;** 40 (right), ©Bachmann/**N E Stock Photo;** 41 (top left), ©**R.T. Nowitz;** 41 (top right), courtesy of Mohamed Maaty; 41 (bottom), ©**Diana Rasche;** 42 (left), ©**Joan Dunlop;** 42 (pebbles), ©**KK&A, Ltd.;** 43 (top), ©**R.T. Nowitz;** 43 (bottom), ©K. Scholz/**H. Armstrong Roberts;** 44, ©Kathleen Campbell/**Tony Stone Images, Inc.;** 45 (left), ©**Robert Holmes;** 45 (sweet potato), ©**KK&S, Ltd.;** 46-47, ©Will & Deni McIntyre/**Tony Stone Images, Inc.;** 48, ©**Photri, Inc.;** 49 (top left), ©**H. Armstrong Roberts;** 49 (mummy image), ©**KK&A, Ltd.;** 49 (bottom), ©**Photri, Inc.;** 50 (left), ©Richard Elliott/**Tony Stone Images, Inc.;** 50 (right), ©Werner Otto/**Tony Stone Images, Inc.;** 51 (top), ©Marc A. Auth/**N E Stock Photo;** 51 (bottom), ©**Richard Nowitz;** 51 (papyrus), ©**KK&A, Ltd.;** 52, ©Steve Vidler/**SuperStock International, Inc.;** 53 (top), ©**H. Armstrong Roberts;** 53 (bottom), ©**Photri, Inc.;** 54 (both pictures), ©**Diana Rasche;** 55 (top), ©**Photri, Inc.;** 55 (bottom), ©**Robert Holmes;** 56 (left), ©Prim and Ray Manley/**SuperStock International, Inc.;** 56 (right), ©**Dave G. Houser;** 57 (left & right), ©**Photri, Inc.;** 57 (middle), ©James Palmer/**Tony Stone Images, Inc.;** 59, ©Kathleen Campbell/**Tony Stone Images, Inc.;** 60 & 61, ©**KK&A, Ltd.**

INDEX

Page numbers in boldface type indicate illustrations

ABOUT THE AUTHOR

R. Conrad Stein was born and grew up in Chicago. After serving in the Marine Corps, he attended the University of Illinois, where he earned a degree in history. The author now lives in Chicago with his wife and their daughter Janna. Mr. Stein has published more than eighty books for young readers, most of them on history and geography.